THE UNOFFICIAL
MASTERBUILT
SMOKER
COOKBOOK

THE ART OF SMOKING MEAT
WITH YOUR ELECTRIC SMOKER

ROGER MURPHY

CONTENTS

FISH, WILD GAME, AND VEGGIES

SMOKING MEAT BASICS

FOOD SAFETY

INTRODUCTION

With clear and concise instructions, this book shows you how to get the most out of your smoker. This book provides detailed instructions on how to smoke meats, seafood, game meats, and veggies, as well as tips on selecting the best cuts of meat and choosing the correct wood chips for flavor. Although the cookbook contains irresistible recipes guaranteed to please, including classic favorites like pulled pork and beef brisket, you'll also find exciting dishes like smoked chicken wings, tuna fillets, and even smoked bbq wild rabbit. Are you looking to perfect your smoked meat game? With clear instructions and easy-to-follow steps, this book will help you take your smoking to the next level. Look no further than this fantastic electric smoker cookbook with everything you need to know about smoking meat, including how to choose the right smoker, what cuts of meat work best, and how to create flavorful recipes that impress you, your friends, and your family. Whether you're a beginner or a seasoned pro, this cookbook is a must-have for any smoker's library!

SMOKING

Smoking is generally used as one of the cooking methods nowadays. With modern cooking techniques, food enriched in protein, such as meat, would spoil if cooked for extended periods. Whereas, Smoking is a low & slow process of cooking meat. Where there is smoke, there is a flavor. With white smoke, you can boost the taste of your food. In addition to this statement, you can also preserve the nutrition in the food. Smoking is flexible & one of the oldest techniques of making food. You must brush the marinade over your food while you cook and let the miracle happen. The only thing you need to do is to add a handful of fresh wood chips when required. Just taste your regular grilled and smoked meat, and you will find the difference. Remember one thing, i.e., "Smoking is an art." With a bit of time & practice, even you can become an expert. Once you become an expert in smoking techniques, you will never look for other cooking techniques. To find which smoking technique works for you, you must experiment with different woods & cooking methods. Just cook the meat over an indirect heat source & cook it for hours. When smoking your meats, you must let the smoke escape & move around.

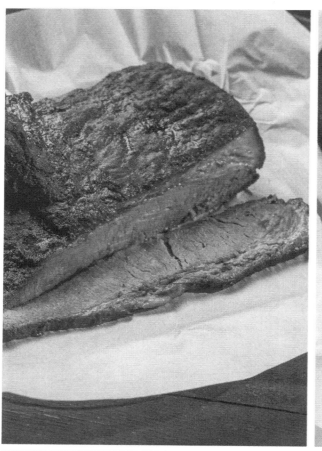

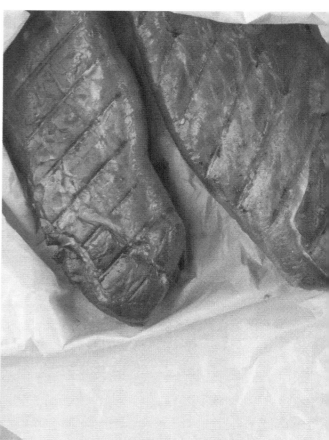

BEEF, PORK, AND HAM

NEW YORK STRIP STEAK WITH BOURBON BUTTER

TOTAL COOK TIME 1 HOUR 30 MINUTES

INGREDIENTS FOR 2 SERVINGS

THE MEAT

- 2 New York strip steaks

THE BUTTER

- Salted butter, room temperature – ½ cup
- Fresh parsley, chopped – 1 tablespoon
- 1 green onion top, minced
- Bourbon – 2 tablespoons
- Smoked paprika – 1 teaspoon

THE SEASONING

- Steak rub

THE SMOKE

- Preheat the electric smoker to 225°f (110°c) using pecan wood chips

METHOD

1. First, prepare the butter. Combine the butter, parsley, green onion, bourbon, and paprika in a small bowl. Transfer to a piece of plastic wrap, shape into a log and roll tightly. Chill until ready to use.
2. Season the steaks with steak rub and place in the smoker. Cook for approximately 60 minutes until the internal temperature registers 130°f (55°c), for medium-rare.
3. Place a skillet over high heat. When the steak is cooked to your liking, sear each piece on both sides in the skillet.
4. Top with a couple slices of bourbon butter and serve straight away.

SMOKED TRI-TIP ROAST

TOTAL COOK TIME 3 HOURS 20 MINUTES

INGREDIENTS FOR 6-8 SERVINGS

THE MEAT

- Tri-tip roast, no fat cap (2.5-lbs, 1.1-kgs)

THE RUB

- Chili powder – 1½ teaspoons
- Sea salt – 2 teaspoons
- Brown sugar – 1 teaspoon
- Black pepper – 1 teaspoon
- Onion powder – 1 teaspoon
- Espresso powder – 1 teaspoon
- Garlic powder – ½ teaspoon

THE SMOKE

- Add a bowl of water to the bottom of the smoker and add cherry wood chips to the side tray. Preheat the electric smoker to 225°f (110°c).

METHOD

1. First, prepare the rub. Combine the chili powder, salt, sugar, pepper, onion powder, espresso powder, and garlic powder.
2. Cover the outside of the roast with the rub, set aside to rest for 45 minutes.
3. Arrange the roast in the center of the smoker and arrange a drip pan on the rack below.
4. Close the door, open the vent and smoke for a couple of hours until the internal temperature registers 135°f (60°c). The wood chips or water may need to be replenished during this time.
5. Take the roast out of the smoker and tent with aluminum foil, set aside for half an hour. Thinly slice and serve.

STICKY SMOKY MEATLOAF

TOTAL COOK TIME 3 HOURS 30 MINUTES

INGREDIENTS FOR 3-4 SERVINGS

THE MEAT

- Lean ground beef (2-lbs, 0.9-kgs)

THE MEATLOAF

- 1 red pepper, minced
- 1 yellow onion, peeled and minced
- 2 cloves garlic, peeled and minced
- BBQ sauce - ⅔ cup
- 1 egg, beaten
- Breadcrumbs – ½ cup
- Salt – 1 teaspoon
- Black pepper – ½ teaspoon
- Cayenne pepper – ¼ teaspoon
- BBQ rub – 3 tablespoons

THE SMOKE

- Add a bowl of water to the bottom of the smoker and add hickory wood chips. Preheat the electric smoker to 250°f (120°c).

METHOD

1. Using clean hands, combine the beef, pepper, onion, garlic, half of the BBQ sauce, egg, breadcrumbs, salt, pepper, and cayenne.
2. Shape the mixture into a loaf and season with BBQ rub. Place in the smoker and cook for approximately 2 hours. At this point, brush the meatloaf with the remaining BBQ sauce. Continue to cook until the internal temperature registers 160°f (70°c). The wood chips or water may need to be replenished during this time.

SUMMER SPICED SAUSAGE

TOTAL COOK TIME 8 HOURS 30 MINUTES

INGREDIENTS FOR 18 SERVINGS

THE MEAT

- Lean hamburger meat (5-lbs, 2.3-kgs)

THE SEASONING

- Meat cure – 5 teaspoons
- Sugar cure – 2 tablespoons
- Liquid smoke -2 teaspoons
- Mustard seeds – 2 teaspoons
- Garlic powder – 1 teaspoon
- Peppercorns – 2 teaspoons
- Red pepper, crushed – 2 teaspoons
- Coarse pepper – 2 teaspoons

THE SMOKE

- Preheat the electric smoker to 225°f (110°c)

METHOD

1. Combine the meat, meat cure, sugar cure, liquid smoke, mustard seeds, garlic, peppercorns, red pepper, and coarse pepper. Transfer the mixture to a resealable container and chill for 2-3 days. Mix the meat at least twice every day.
2. Form the mixture into 2-ins (5-cms) and place in the smoker. Cook for approximately 8 hours until the internal temperature registers 160°f (70°c).

*Plus 3 days standing time.

TEXAN BEEF BRISKET

TOTAL COOK TIME 16 HOURS 30 MINUTES

INGREDIENTS FOR 18 SERVINGS

THE MEAT

- 1 whole packer brisket, chilled (12-lbs, 5.5-kgs)

THE SEASONING

- Garlic powder – 2 tablespoons
- Salt – 2 tablespoons
- Black pepper – 2 tablespoons

THE SMOKE

- Preheat the smoker to 225°f (110°c) using hardwood smoke and indirect heat.

METHOD

1. Arrange the brisket so the point end is underneath. Cut away and discard any excess fat.
2. Trim down the crescent-shaped fat section to ensure a smooth transition between point and flat. Trim any excess fat from the point. Square the ends and edges of the flat.
3. Flip the brisket and trim the fat cap down to a ¼-ins (0.6-cms) thick.
4. In a small bowl, combine the garlic, salt, and pepper. Sprinkle the mixture over the whole brisket.
5. Arrange the brisket in the smoker with the point end facing the heat source. Close the lid and cook for approximately 8 hours until the internal temperature registers 165°f (75°c).
6. Roll out a piece of butcher paper and arrange the brisket in the center. Wrap the paper around the brisket securely so that it is leak-proof. Return the parcel to the smoker and arrange seam side down. Close the smoker lid and continue to cook until the internal temperature registers 200°f (95°c). This will take approximately 6-7 hours.
7. Allow the cooked meat to rest for an hour before slicing and serving against the grain.

SMOKED BEEF RIBS

TOTAL COOK TIME 9 HOURS 15 MINUTES

INGREDIENTS FOR 4 SERVINGS

THE MEAT

- 4-bone section beef ribs (4-lb, 1.8-kg)

THE INGREDIENTS

- Horseradish flavor Dijon mustard, any brand – 2 tablespoons
- Beef rub, any brand – 6 tablespoons

THE SPRITZ

- Hot sauce, any brand – ¼ cup
- White vinegar - 1 cup'

THE SMOKE

- Add Hickory or oak wood chips to the wood tray.
- Set the electric smoker to 250°F (120°C) for indirect cooking

METHOD

1. Cover the beef ribs with the flavored mustard, and season generously all over with beef rub.
2. Transfer the ribs to the preheated smoker, and insert a meat thermometer, programmed to 200°F (95°C) in the thickest part of the ribs while not touching the bone. Close the smoker's lid and smoke the ribs for 3 hours.
3. Add the hot sauce and white vinegar to a spray bottle and shake to combine.
4. Once the ribs have smoked for 3 hours, start to spritz them every 40-60 minutes. Continue to smoke until they register an internal temperature of 200°F (95°C). The whole smoking process will take approximately 8-10 hours.
5. Take the beef ribs out of the smoker and wrap them in aluminum foil. Set aside to rest in an insulated cooler for a minimum of 60 minutes before slicing

APPLE SMOKED PORK LOIN

TOTAL COOK TIME 4 HOURS 50 MINUTES

INGREDIENTS FOR 8 SERVINGS

THE MEAT

- Whole boneless pork loin (6-lbs, 2.3-kgs)

THE RUB

- Chines 5-spice powder – 1 tablespoon
- Sea salt – 2 teaspoons
- Freshly cracked black pepper – 1 teaspoon
- Garlic powder – ½ teaspoon
- Nutmeg _ ¼ teaspoon
- Safflower oil – 1 tablespoon

THE SMOKE

- Preheat the electric smoker to 225°f (110°c) using oak wood chips
- Add a 50/50 apple juice and water mix in the bowl of our smoker base.
- Add apple wood chips to the tray

METHOD

1. First, rinse the pork loin in cool water. Pat dry with kitchen paper towels.
2. Trim off excess fat or silver skin leaving a ¼ -ins (0.62-cms) of fat on the meat.
3. Transfer the loin to a sheet pan.
4. In a bowl, combine the Chinese 5-spice powder with the sea salt, cracked black pepper, garlic powder, nutmeg, and oil.
5. Rub the spice mix all over the pork loin and allow the meat to rest at room temperature for up to 1 hour.
6. Put the pork inside the smoker on the middle rack, fat side facing upwards. Close the door and set the timer for 3 hours.
7. When the pork has been smoking for 2 hours, check the meat. It needs to read an internal temperature of 155°F (70°C).
8. Check the pork every 45 minutes, adding additional wood chips as necessary.
9. When the pork is smoked to the correct temperature, transfer it to a chopping board and tent with foil.
10. Set the meat aside to rest for 20 minutes.
11. Slice, and serve with slaw.

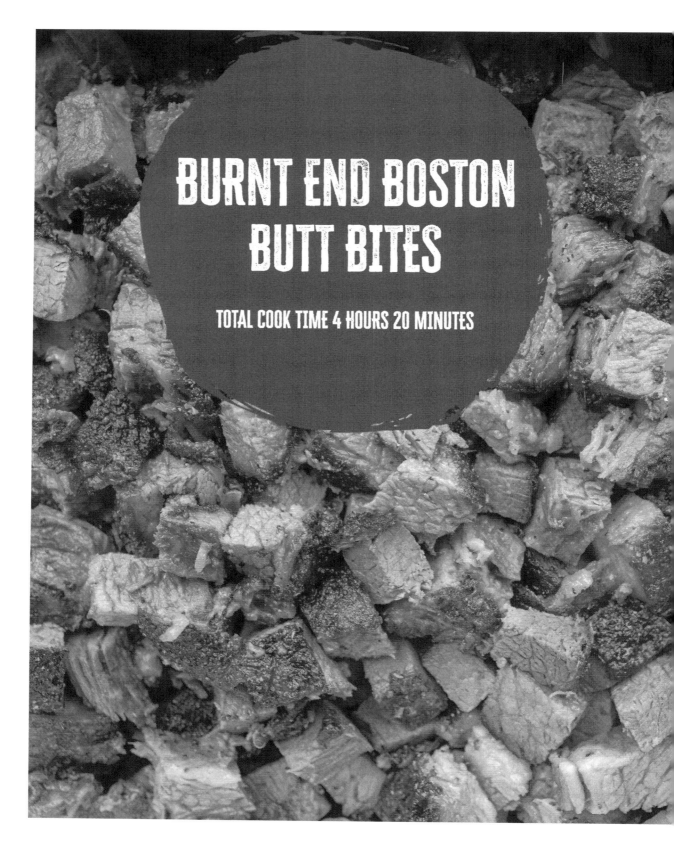

BURNT END BOSTON BUTT BITES

TOTAL COOK TIME 4 HOURS 20 MINUTES

INGREDIENTS FOR 8-10 SERVINGS

THE MEAT

- Boneless Boston butt, fat trimmed (4-lbs, 1.8-kgs)

THE RUB

- Mustard, to taste
- BBQ rub, of choice

THE INGREDIENTS

- Butter – 6 pats
- Honey, to taste
- BBQ sauce, to season
- Brown sugar, to sweeten

THE SMOKE

- Preheat the electric smoker to 250°F (120°C)

METHOD

1. Add the pork to an aluminum pan and coat with mustard and rub.
2. Smoke in the electric smoker for between 2-3 hours, or until an internal thermometer registers 160°F (70°C).
3. Cut the meat into (1-ins, 2.5-cms) cubes and place in a second aluminum pan.
4. Pour the majority of the juice over the pork along with 6 pats of butter.
5. Drizzle with honey along with the BBQ sauce, to taste. Scatter brown sugar over the top.
6. Using aluminum foil, wrap the top of the pan and smoke for an additional 1 ½ hours.
7. Remove the aluminum foil and stir. Drain off any excess juice and drizzle with additional BBQ sauce.
8. Turn the temperature of your smoker up to 275°F (135°C) and smoke for half an hour, until the sauce is caramelized.
9. Stir, serve and enjoy.

PORK TENDERLOIN BRUSCHETTA

TOTAL COOK TIME 3 HOURS 15 MINUTES

INGREDIENTS FOR 8-10 SERVINGS

THE MEAT

- Pork tenderloin (2-lbs, 0.9-kgs)

THE INGREDIENTS

- Sea salt, to season
- Freshly ground black pepper, to season
- Garlic salt
- Bruschetta, toasted, sliced
- Pimento cheese dip, store-bought
- Jarred mild jalapeno peppers

THE SMOKE

- Preheat the electric smoker to 225°F (110°C)
- Add hickory wood chips

METHOD

1. Season both sides of the pork with sea salt, freshly ground black pepper, and garlic salt to taste.
2. Place the tenderloin on the smoker and smoke for 1½ hours or until an internal thermometer registers 150°F (65°C).
3. Remove the meat from the smoker and using heavy aluminum foil, wrap.
4. Return to the smoker for an additional ½ hours or until a thermometer registers 165°F (75°F).
5. When the tenderloin has finished smoking, remove the meat from the smoker and slice into tenderloins approximately ¼-ins (0.65-cms). Cut the pork medallions in half.
6. Add a medallion to a slice of Bruschetta toast and top with a spoon full of pimento cheese and jalapeno pepper.
7. Serve and enjoy.

SMOKED CHORIZO QUESO

TOTAL COOK TIME 1 HOURS 10 MINUTES

INGREDIENTS FOR 4 SERVINGS

THE MEAT

- Chorizo (1-lbs, 0.5-kgs)

THE INGREDIENTS

- Processed cheese, cubed (1-lbs,0.45-kgs)
- Cream cheese, cubed – ½ cup
- Canned tomatoes and chili (10-ozs, 285-gms)
- Tortilla chips, to serve

THE SMOKE

- Preheat the electric smoker to 250°F (120°C)
- Add apple wood chips

METHOD

1. In a skillet or frying pan, cook the chorizo and drain the grease.
2. In a disposable aluminum, tray combine the processed cheese with the cream cheese, canned tomatoes, and cooked chorizo.
3. Smoke in the smoker for 60 minutes, until entirely melted, mixing every 20 minutes.
4. Serve with tortilla chips.

SMOKED PORK RIBS

TOTAL COOK TIME 5 HOURS 5 MINUTES

INGREDIENTS FOR 8 SERVINGS
THE MEAT

- Pork ribs (4-lbs, 1.8-kgs)

THE RUB

- Salt – ½ tablespoon
- Brown sugar – ¼ cup
- Chili powder- 2½ teaspoons
- Ground cumin – 1½ tablespoons
- Cayenne pepper – 2 teaspoons
- Freshly ground black pepper – 2 teaspoon
- Garlic powder – 2 teaspoons
- Onion powder – 2 teaspoons

THE SMOKE

- Preheat the electric smoker to 225°F (110°C)
- Add hickory wood chips to the smoker

METHOD

1. In a bowl, combine the salt, brown sugar, chili powder, cumin, cayenne pepper, black pepper, garlic powder, and onion powder.
2. Rub the g mix all over the pork and set aside for 2 hours, before smoking. This will also allow the meat to come to room temperature.
3. Smoke the ribs in the smoker for 3 hours, using the hickory chips for the first 2 hours only.
4. After 3 hours have elapsed remove the ribs from the smoker and wrap in heavy aluminum foil and cook for an additional 1-1½ hours.
5. Serve the ribs and enjoy.

PEACH BARBECUE PULLED PORK

TOTAL COOK TIME 5 HOURS 15 MINUTES

INGREDIENTS FOR 20 SERVINGS

THE MEAT

- Pork shoulder (10-lb, 4.5-kg)

THE INGREDIENTS

- Pork rub, any brand – 1 cup
- Peach BBQ sauce, any brand, as needed
- 20 sandwich buns, split
- Coleslaw, as needed

THE SMOKE

- Set the electric smoker for indirect cooking to 250-275°F (120-135°C)
- Hickory or pecan wood chips work well for this recipe

METHOD

1. Using kitchen paper towels, pat the meat dry.
2. Take a sharp knife and make cuts all over the surface of the butt. Scatter the pork rub over the pork, pressing it gently into the meat.
3. Cook the meat on indirect cooking at around 250-275°F (120-135°C).
4. Cook the pork for around 5 hours, or until the internal temperature of the meat registers an internal temperature of 195-205°F (90-95°C) until the meat falls apart.
5. Remove from the smoker and set aside to rest for 20 minutes before shredding.
6. Mix 10 cups of sauce into the pulled, shredded pork.
7. Cook until heated through.
8. Serve the pulled pork in the sandwich buns topped with coleslaw.
9. Enjoy.

BROWN SUGAR & MUSTARD GLAZED HAM

TOTAL COOK TIME 6 HOURS 30 MINUTES

INGREDIENTS FOR 10-12 SERVINGS

THE MEAT

- Bone-in, pre-cooked ham (8-lbs, 3.7-kgs)

THE RUB

- Onion powder – 2 teaspoons
- Garlic powder – 1 teaspoon
- Dried rosemary leaves – 1 teaspoon
- Dried thyme leaves – 1 teaspoon
- Sweet paprika – 2 teaspoons
- Kosher salt – ½ teaspoon
- Freshly ground black pepper – ½ teaspoon
- Brown sugar – 2 tablespoons
- Olive oil – 1-2 tablespoons
- Honey mustard, to brush

THE GLAZE

- Orange juice – 1 cup
- Pineapple juice – 1 cup
- Runny honey – ½ cup
- Honey mustard – ¼ cup
- Ground cloves – ¼ teaspoon
- Ground ginger – 1 teaspoon
- Firmly packed brown sugar – 2 cups

THE SMOKE

- Preheat smoker to 225°f (110°c)
- Add the wood chips, refilling when needed

METHOD

1. Take the ham out of the fridge and using kitchen paper towels, pat dry.
2. Place the ham on a baking sheet.
3. In a bowl, combine the onion powder together with the garlic powder, rosemary, thyme, paprika, salt, pepper, brown sugar and 1 tbsp of olive oil. Whisk thoroughly to achieve a silky smooth paste. You may add additional oil if needed.
4. Rub the surface of the ham with the paste and set aside to rest for 60 minutes at room temperature.
5. In a pan, combine the orange juice, pineapple juice with the honey, mustards, cloves, ginger, and cardamom. Heat over moderate to low heat. Stirring frequently until the mixture is entirely blended and warmed through. Turn the heat down to low.
6. Brush the ham with the honey-mustard mixture and transfer to the smoker, cooking for 60 minutes, without lifting the smoker's lid.
7. After 60 minutes, open the smoker and baste the ham with a little of the glaze.
8. Close the smoker lid and continue cooking for between 4-6 hours, remembering to baste every 45 minutes.
9. When the internal temperature of the ham registers 125°F (50°C), combine 3-4 tablespoons of the remaining glaze with the brown sugar to create a honey-like consistency. Whisk until entirely smooth.
10. Brush the paste over the top of the ham, allowing it to drip down the sides of the ham, covering the majority of the surface.
11. Continue smoking until the ham reaches an internal temperature of 145°F (65°C). There should be a sweet crust on the surface of the ham.
12. Remove from the smoker and set aside for half an hour before slicing.

PINEAPPLE-HONEY HAM

TOTAL COOK TIME 12 HOURS 30 MINUTES

INGREDIENTS FOR 8 SERVINGS

THE MEAT

- 1 bone-in ready to eat ham (6-lbs, 2.7-kgs)

THE SEASONING

- Smoked paprika – 1 tablespoon
- Cayenne pepper – ½ teaspoon
- Salt – 2 teaspoons
- Sugar – 1 tablespoon
- Mustard powder – 1 teaspoon
- Olive oil

THE BASTE

- Pineapple juice – ¾ cup
- Chicken stock – ¾ cup
- Mustard powder – ½ teaspoon
- Vegetable oil – 2 tablespoons
- Ground cloves - pinch

THE GLAZE

- Pineapple juice – ¼ cup
- Honey – ½ cup
- Ground cloves - pinch
- Mustard powder – ½ teaspoon

THE SMOKE

- When ready to smoke, preheat the electric smoker to 235°f (115°c) using hickory wood chips in the side tray and adding water to the bowl

METHOD

1. Score the top of the ham in a criss-cross pattern using a sharp knife.
2. Prepare the seasoning; combine the paprika, cayenne, salt, sugar, and mustard powder.
3. Brush the ham with a light coating of oil and season with the spice mix. Cover and chill overnight.
4. The day you wish to cook the ham, prepare the baste. Add the pineapple juice, stock, mustard, vegetable oil, and cloves to a saucepan over moderate heat until thickened.
5. Place the ham in the smoker and cook for 4-5 hours until the internal temperature registers 140°f (70°c).
6. Just before the final hour of cooking, prepare the glaze. Combine the pineapple juice, honey, cloves, and mustard. Brush the glaze mixture over the ham a few times for the final hour of cooking.

CHERRY BOURBON SMOKED HAM

TOTAL COOK TIME 12 HOURS 30 MINUTES

INGREDIENTS FOR 3-4 SERVINGS

THE MEAT

- 1 pre-cooked ham (9-lbs, 4-kgs)

THE RUB

- Whole cloves
- Cherry meat rub – 4 tablespoons
- Cherry preserves - 1⅛ cups
- Bourbon - ⅔ cup
- Allspice – ¾ teaspoon
- Fresh thyme, chopped – 1 tablespoon
- Salt and black pepper
- Molasses – ½ cup

THE SMOKE

- Preheat the electric smoker to 225°f (110°c) using cherry wood chips and prepare for indirect cooking

METHOD

1. Using a sharp knife, score the ham with a diamond pattern slicing a ¼-ins (0.6-cms) deep. Arrange a clove in the center of each diamond shape. Season with cherry meat rub.
2. Place the ham in the smoker and cook until the internal temperature registers 130°f (55°c).
3. Half an hour or so before the ham is finished cooking, add the preserves, bourbon, allspice, thyme, salt, black pepper, and molasses to a saucepan over moderately low heat and simmer for 25 minutes before thick and sticky.
4. When the ham reaches 130°f (55°c), glaze the ham with the bourbon/cherry glaze every 25 minutes until the meat registers an internal temperature of 140°f (60°c).
5. Slice and serve!

SMOKED HAM HOCKS

TOTAL COOK TIME 4 HOURS 30 MINUTES

INGREDIENTS FOR 6 SERVINGS

THE MEAT

- 3 ham hocks

THE BRINE

- Filtered water, boiling hot – 16 cups
- Brown sugar – ½ cup
- Salt – 1 cup
- Black peppercorns – 1 teaspoon
- 2 bay leaves

THE SMOKE

- When ready to smoke, preheat the electric smoker to 250°f (120°c) using hickory wood chips in the side tray and adding water to the bowl

METHOD

1. First, prepare the brine. Add the boiling water to a deep pot along with the sugar, salt, peppercorns, and bay leaves. Stir to dissolve the sugar and salt then set aside to cool completely.
2. Add the ham hocks to extra large resealable ziplock bags and arrange in a dish. Carefully pour the brine into the bag(s) to cover and seal. Chill for 24 hours. Remove the hocks from the brine, rinse well and pat dry with paper towels.
3. Arrange a rack inside a sheet pan and place the hocks on top. Chill for another 24 hours.
4. Place the hocks in the smoker and cook with the vent open for 2-4 hours. You'll need to replenish the water and wood chips every hour.
5. The hocks are cooked when their internal temperature registers 160°f (80°c).

*Plus two days brining time.

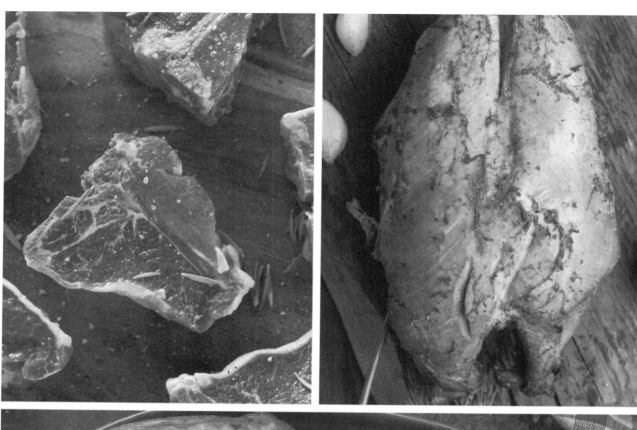
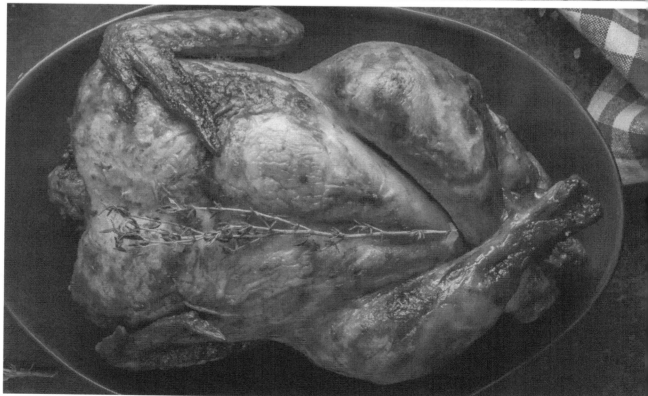

LAMB AND POULTRY

GREEK-STYLE LEG OF LAMB

TOTAL COOK TIME 6 HOURS 30 MINUTES

INGREDIENTS FOR 4 SERVINGS

THE MEAT

- 1 boneless leg of lamb (2.-lbs, 0.9-kgs)

THE RUB

- 4 cloves garlic, peeled, minced
- Olive oil – 2 tablespoons
- Salt – 2 teaspoons
- Freshly ground black pepper – 1 teaspoon
- Oregano – 2 tablespoons
- Thyme – 1 teaspoon

THE SMOKE

- Preheat the electric smoker to 250°f (120°c)
- Add the wood chips

METHOD

1. Trim the lamb of excess fat and trim while keeping the meat an even thickness. You may need to tie the lamb up with kitchen twine.
2. In a bowl, combine the garlic with the oil, salt, black pepper, oregano, and thyme. Rub the mixture all over the lamb.
3. Transfer the lamb to a serving dish and cover with kitchen wrap. Transfer to the fridge to marinate for a minimum of 60 minutes.
4. Place the lamb on the smoker rack and smoke for between 3-4 hours or until the internal temperature of the meat registers 145°F (65°C).
5. Remove from the smoker, slice and serve.

LAMB BURGERS WITH ROSEMARY AIOLI

TOTAL COOK TIME 1 HOUR 15 MINUTES

INGREDIENTS FOR 4 SERVINGS

THE MEAT

- 1 bone-in ready to eat ham (6-lbs, 2.7-kgs)

THE BURGERS

- Salt and pepper
- 4 burger buns

THE AIOLI

- Mayonnaise - ⅓ cup
- Lemon juice – 1 tablespoon
- Dijon mustard – 1 teaspoon
- Fresh rosemary, minced – 1 teaspoon
- 2 garlic cloves – peeled, minced
- Black pepper - pinch
- Salt - ⅛ teaspoon

THE SMOKE

- Preheat the electric smoker to 250°f (120°c) and prepare for indirect cooking

METHOD

1. Season the meat well and shape into 4 equal patties.
2. Place the patties in the smoker over indirect heat and cook for approximately 45 minutes until the internal temperature registers 165°f (75°c).
3. In the meantime, prepare the aioli. Combine the mayonnaise, lemon juice, mustard, rosemary, garlic, pepper, and salt in a small bowl.
4. Serve the cooked burgers in the buns topped with aioli.

MOROCCAN LAMB RIBS

TOTAL COOK TIME 3 HOURS 20 MINUTES

INGREDIENTS FOR 4 SERVINGS

THE MEAT

- 2 racks of lamb, membrane removed

THE RUB

- Paprika – 2 tablespoons
- Coriander seeds – ½ tablespoon
- Kosher salt – ½ tablespoon
- Cumin seeds – 1 teaspoon
- Ground allspice- 1 teaspoon
- Powdered lemon peel – 1 teaspoon
- Ground black pepper – ½ teaspoons

THE SMOKE

- Preheat the electric smoker to 250°f (120°c) for indirect cooking
- Add your choice of wood chips

METHOD

1. Combine the paprika followed by the coriander seeds, kosher salt, cumin seeds, ground allspice, lemon peel, and black pepper and using a pestle and mortar grind the seasonings into a powder.
2. Season both sides of the lamb liberally with the rub.
3. Transfer to your smoker, cover and cook for 3 hours until tender.
4. Remove from the smoker and serve.

SMOKED LAMB SHOULDER CHOPS

TOTAL COOK TIME 4 HOURS 30 MINUTES

INGREDIENTS FOR 4 SERVINGS

THE MEAT

- 4 thick lamb shoulder chops
- Olive oil
- Texas style rub of choice

THE BRINE

- Buttermilk – 4 cups
- Cold water – 1 cup
- Coarse kosher salt – ¼ cup

THE SMOKE

- Preheat the electric smoker to 240°f (115°c)
- Fill the smoker's water pan with hot water
- Add cherry or apple wood chips

METHOD

1. Prepare the brine: Add the buttermilk along with the water to a large jug. Add the salt and stir for 30 seconds until the salt is entirely dissolved.
2. Add the chops to a Ziplock bag and pour the buttermilk mixture over the chops, to cover.
3. Transfer the ziplock bag to the fridge for 3-4 hours.
4. Remove the chops from the ziplock bag, discard the brine and rinse the chops with cold water. Set to one side.
5. Drizzle a drop of oil over the top side of the chops, using a pastry brush to cover.
6. Scatter a generous amount of Texas-style rub over the top side of the chops.
7. Turn the meat over and repeat the oil and Texas rub process.
8. Add the lamb chops to the smoker and smoke for approximately 25 minutes. Cooking time will depend on the thickness of the meat.
9. The chops are sufficiently cooked when an internal thermometer registers 110°F (45°C) transfer to an extremely hot grill to finish.

SPICY LAMB SAUSAGES WITH HONEY MUSTARD

TOTAL COOK TIME 3 HOURS 15 MINUTES

INGREDIENTS FOR 4 SERVINGS

THE MEAT

- Spicy lamb sausages, room temperature (2½-lbs, 1.1-kgs)

THE HONEY MUSTARD

- Honey – ¼ cup
- Mayonnaise – ¼ cup
- Mustard – ¼ cup
- White vinegar – 1 tablespoon
- Cayenne pepper – ¼ teaspoon

THE SMOKE

- Preheat the electric smoker to 250°f (120°c) using apple wood chips, fill the water pan half full

METHOD

1. Arrange the sausages on the smoker spaced apart a little.
2. Smoke for 3 hours with the vent open until the sausages reach an internal temperature of 165°f (75°c). The wood chips and water will need replacing ever hour.
3. In the meantime, prepare the honey mustard. Combine the honey, mayonnaise, mustard, vinegar, and cayenne pepper in a small bowl.
4. Serve the cooked sausages with the honey mustard.

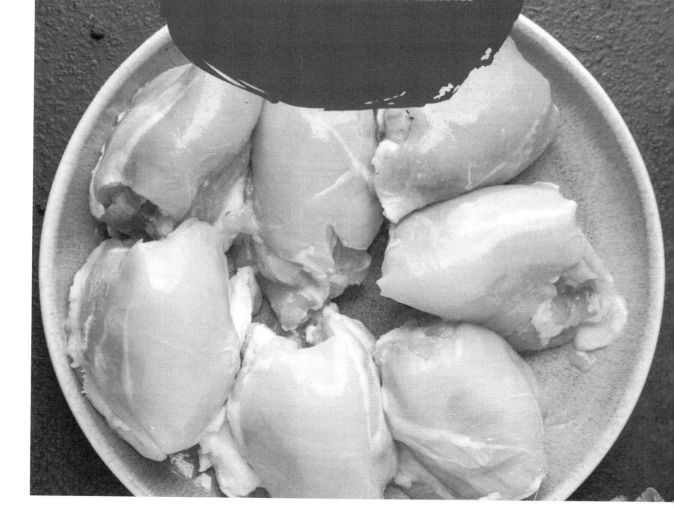

BUFFALO CHICKEN DIP

TOTAL COOK TIME 3 HOURS 15 MINUTES

INGREDIENTS FOR 6-8 SERVINGS

THE MEAT

- 8 chicken thighs

THE INGREDIENTS

- Chicken rub, of choice
- Cream cheese (16-ozs, 460-gms)
- Cheddar cheese, shredded – 2 cups
- Ranch dressing – 1 cup
- Hot sauce, of choice – 1½ cups
- 10 slices of bacon, chopped
- Salt and black pepper, to taste
- Hot sauce, to drizzle
- Tortilla chips, to serve

THE SMOKE

- Preheat the electric smoker to 275°F (135°C)

METHOD

1. Season the chicken with chicken rub.
2. Place the chicken in the smoker until the temperature registers 165°F (75°C) for between 2½-3hours.
3. In a bowl, combine the cream cheese, 1½ cups of Cheddar cheese, Ranch dressing and hot sauce, whisking until smooth.
4. Cook the bacon, until crispy and add it to the dip mixture.
5. In a food processor, shred the chicken and add it to the dip.
6. Top with the remaining Cheddar cheese and drizzle with a splash of hot sauce.
7. Smoke in the electric smoker at 275°F (135°C) for between 30-45 minutes.
8. Serve with tortilla chips.

SWEET 'N' SPICY CHICKEN WINGS

TOTAL COOK TIME 11 HOURS 15 MINUTES

INGREDIENTS FOR 3-4 SERVINGS

THE MEAT

- 12 chicken wings

THE SEASONING

- Chicken rub – 2-3 tablespoons
- Baking powder – 1 tablespoon

THE INGREDIENTS

- Spicy BBQ sauce, store-bought – ¼ cup
- Runny honey – ½ cup
- Apple juice – 2-4 tablespoons

THE SMOKE

- Preheat the electric smoker to 225°F (110°C)
- Add the wood chips

METHOD

1. In a bowl, combine the chicken rub with the baking powder and add to a ziplock bag along with the 12 chicken wings and shake the bag to coat.
2. Place the wings on a tray and put in the fridge, overnight.
3. Add the wings to your smoker and smoke for 1½ hours.
4. Flip the chicken wings over and smoke for an additional 1½ hours.
5. While the wings smoke, prepare the sauce by adding the BBQ sauce to a pan along with the runny honey and apple juice and simmer for 5-10 minutes, until it begins to thicken.
6. When the second 1 ½ hours have elapsed check the wings internal temperature. If it is not registering 165°F (75°C) smoke for an additional 30 minutes. The total cooking time will be approximately 2 hours 15 minutes.
7. Remove from the smoker and toss in the sauce.

PERI-PERI CHICKEN

TOTAL COOK TIME 11 HOURS 15 MINUTES

INGREDIENTS FOR 3 SERVINGS

THE MEAT

- 3 chicken breasts, boneless

THE PERI PERI SAUCE

- Red bell pepper, chopped (3½ -ozs, 200-gms)
- Dry red chili – 3⅓ tablespoons
- Paprika – 1 tablespoon
- Vinegar – 1 cup
- Virgin olive oil – 1 cup
- Lime zest – 1 teaspoon
- Onion, peeled, chopped – 3 ½ tablespoons
- 11 garlic cloves, peeled
- Ground black pepper – 1 teaspoon
- Salt - 1 teaspoon
- Oregano – 1 tablespoon
- Freshly squeezed lemon juice – 1 tablespoon
- Honey – 2 tablespoons

THE BRINE

- Water – 16 cups
- Kosher salt – 1 cup
- Brown sugar – ½ cup

THE SMOKE

- Preheat your electric smoker to 280°F (140°C)
- Add wood chips

METHOD

1. To prepare the Peri-Peri sauce, in a food blender combine the bell pepper with the dry chili, paprika, vinegar, virgin olive oil, lime zest, onion, garlic, ground black pepper, salt, oregano, and lemon juice. Process to a paste.
2. Transfer the past to pan and on low cook for 15 minutes.
3. Remove from the heat and allow to completely cool before using.
4. Once cool transfer to a re-sealable jar until ready to use.
5. In the meantime, prepare the brine. Add the water, salt, and brown sugar to a pot and stir until the sugar is entirely dissolved.
6. Add the chicken and transfer to the fridge, overnight.
7. The following day, remove the chicken from the brine and pat dry with kitchen paper towels.
8. Score the chicken approximately ½ -ins (1.25-cms) wide and ¼ -ins (0.62-cms) deep.
9. Transfer the chicken to your smoker. You will need to add additional chips to the smoker after 45 minutes.
10. While the chicken is smoking add the homemade Peri-Peri sauce and honey to a mixing bowl and stir to combine.
11. When the chicken registers an internal temperature of 155°F (70°C) spread the Peri-Peri sauce to the top side of the chicken.
12. As soon as the chicken reaches 165°F (75°C) flip the chicken over and apply another layer of Peri Peri sauce.
13. The chicken is cooked when it registers 165°F (75°C). The total smoking time will be approximately 1½ hours.

HERB-RUBBED APPLE SMOKED TURKEY

TOTAL COOK TIME 6 HOURS 40 MINUTES

INGREDIENTS FOR 8-10 SERVINGS

THE MEAT

- 1 whole turkey, prepared (14-lbs, 6.4-kgs)

THE SEASONING MIX

- Dried thyme – 2 tablespoons
- Powdered sage – 1 tablespoon
- Dried oregano – 2 teaspoons
- Paprika – 2 teaspoons
- Sea salt – 2 teaspoons
- Freshly ground black pepper – 1½ teaspoons
- Dried rosemary -1 teaspoon
- Garlic powder – 1 teaspoon

THE RUB

- Extra-virgin olive oil – ¼ cup
- Freshly squeezed zest of ½ orange

THE SMOKE

- Preheat the electric smoker to 225°F (110°C)
- Add approximately ½ cup each of apple cider and water to the water pan in the bottom of your smoker, until half filled
- Arrange a drip pan on the shelf above the water pan
- Fill the drawer with apple smoker wood chips

METHOD

1. In a bowl, combine the thyme, sage, oregano, paprika, sea salt, black pepper, dried rosemary, and garlic powder.
2. Rub the bird's cavity with ⅓ of the seasoning mix.
3. Add the olive oil along with the orange zest to the remaining ⅔ of the seasoning mix and rub all over the turkey's surface.
4. Tuck the turkey's wingtip tightly underneath the bird and place it on the smoker's middle rack. Close the smoker door and set the timer for 6 ½ hours. The bird needs to smoke for 30-40 minutes for every 1-lbs (0.5-kgs) until its internal temperature on a meat thermometer registers 165°F (75°C). You will, however, need to check every 60 minutes for smoke, add more wood chips if necessary.
5. Check the turkey's internal temperature after 3 hours and every 45 minutes thereafter using a meat thermometer.
6. Transfer the turkey to a chopping board and set aside to rest for between 20-120 minutes, before carving.

EASIEST BBQ SMOKED TURKEY WINGS

TOTAL COOK TIME 12 HOURS 30 MINUTES

INGREDIENTS FOR 3-4 SERVINGS

THE MEAT

- 6 turkey wings, wing tips discarded

THE SEASONING

- Salt and black pepper
- BBQ sauce of choice

THE SMOKE

- Preheat the electric smoker to 225°f (110°c) using cherry wood chips and prepare for indirect cooking

METHOD

1. Season the turkey wings with salt and pepper and marinade in BBQ sauce overnight.
2. Remove the turkey wings from the marinade and place in the hot smoker. Smoke until the internal temperature registers 165°f (75°c). Baste the wings with more BBQ sauce when they are almost done.
3. Allow to rest for 10 minutes before serving with additional BBQ sauce on the side.

WHITE WINE TURKEY DOGS

TOTAL COOK TIME 2 HOURS

INGREDIENTS FOR 10 SERVINGS

THE MEAT

- 10 turkey hot dogs

THE HOT DOGS

- Butter – 4 tablespoons
- Mushrooms, chopped – 3 cups
- 1 green pepper, seeded and sliced
- 1 yellow onion, peeled and sliced
- 1 bottle white wine
- 10 hot dog buns

THE SMOKE

- Preheat the electric smoker to 225°f (110°c) using peach wood chips

METHOD

1. Add the butter, mushrooms, green pepper, onion, and white wine to a baking tin.
2. Arrange the baking tin on a lower rack in the smoker and arrange the sausages on the rack above. Smoke for 40 minutes, then add the sausages to the wine mixture. Smoke for another 40 minutes.
3. Arrange the cooked sausages in the buns and top with a little of the cooked mushroom, pepper, and onion. Serve straight away.

FISH, WILD GAME, AND VEGGIES

HALIBUT WITH HOMEMADE TARTAR SAUCE

TOTAL COOK TIME 7 HOURS 15 MINUTES

INGREDIENTS FOR 4 SERVINGS

THE FISH

- Halibut (2-lbs, 0.9-kgs)

THE RUB

- Brown sugar – ¼ cup
- Granulated sugar – ¼ cup
- Kosher salt – ½ cup
- Ground coriander – 1 teaspoon

THE TARTAR SAUCE

- White onion, minced – 2 tablespoons
- Tomatoes, diced – ¼ cup
- Dill pickled, diced – 2 tablespoons
- Mayonnaise – ½ cup
- Jarred vinegar from hot pepper jar – 2 teaspoons
- Salt, to taste

THE SMOKE

- Preheat the electric smoker to 200°F (95°C)
- Add orange smoker wood chips

METHOD

1. First, in a bowl combine the brown sugar with the granulated sugar along with the kosher salt and coriander.
2. Rub the seasoning all over the fish.
3. Wrap the fish in kitchen wrap and arrange on a rimmed baking sheet and transfer to the fridge, to brine for 3 hours.
4. Remove the kitchen wrap and rinse the fish. Using kitchen paper towel, pat dry.
5. Set the catfish on a drying rack set over a sheet pan and place in the fridge for 1-2 hours.
6. Remove from the fridge and cook in the smoker until the internal temperature registers 140°F (60°C) for approximately 2 hours.
7. For the tartar sauce, combine the white onion with the tomatoes, dill pickle, mayonnaise, and pepper vinegar, and season with salt, to taste.

GARLIC DILL SALMON

TOTAL COOK TIME 20 HOURS 15 MINUTES

INGREDIENTS FOR 12 SERVINGS

THE FISH

- 2 large salmon fillets, pin bones removed

THE BRINE

- Water – 2 cups
- Brown sugar – 1 cup
- Kosher salt - ⅓ cup

THE SEASONING

- Garlic, peeled and minced – 3 tablespoons
- Fresh dill, chopped – 1 tablespoon

THE SMOKE

- While the smoker is cold, add alder wood chips to the wood tray
  Set the electric smoker to 180°F (80°C)
- When the smoker has reached the desired temperature, put an additional batch of wood chips in the wood chip tray
- Fill the water pan to the level recommended in the smoker manual

METHOD

1. In a bowl, thoroughly combine the brine ingredients (water, brown sugar, and kosher salt).
2. Place the fish in the brine, and transfer to the fridge for 16 hours.
3. Remove the salmon from the brine, rinse under cold running water, and, using paper towels, pat dry. Allow the fish to rest uncovered on a rack in the fridge for 2-4 hours until a pellicle forms.
4. Season the fish with garlic and fresh dill.
5. Place the salmon on the rack and smoke the fish in the preheated smoker for 4 hours
6. Remove the fish from the smoker and serve.
7. Enjoy.

PEACH-SMOKED AHI TUNA STEAKS

TOTAL COOK TIME 6 HOURS 20 MINUTES

INGREDIENTS FOR 6 SERVINGS

THE FISH

- 6 Ahi tuna steaks (6-ozs, 170-gms each)

THE MARINADE

- Kosher salt – 3 tablespoons
- Light brown sugar – 3 tablespoons

THE INGREDIENTS

- Extra-virgin olive oil – ¼ cup
- Lemon pepper seasoning shake
- Ground garlic – 1 teaspoon
- 1 fresh lemon, cut into 12 thin slices

THE SMOKE

- Preheat the electric smoker to 190°F (90°C)
- Add water to your smoker pan and place peach woods chip in the smoker tray

METHOD

1. Coat the tuna with the salt and sugar on all sides and place in a ziplock bag. Transfer to the fridge for 4 hours.
2. Remove the tuna steaks from the bag and wipe off the majority of the dry brine.
3. Coat both sides of the tuna steaks with extra-virgin olive oil, lemon pepper seasoning and garlic powder.
4. Place the steaks onto the smoker rack.
5. Arrange 2 slices of fresh lemon on top of each steak. Return the rack to the smoker and smoke for 60-105 minutes or until an internal thermometer registers a heat of 140°F (60°C).
6. Remove the steaks to a chopping board and set aside to rest for 2-3 minutes.
7. Serve and enjoy.

KING CRAB LEGS

TOTAL COOK TIME 55 MINUTES

INGREDIENTS FOR 4 SERVINGS

THE SEAFOOD

- King crab legs (5-lbs, 2.3-kgs)

THE INGREDIENTS

- Butter – 1 cup
- Freshly squeezed lemon juice – ¼ cup
- Lemon pepper seasoning – 2 tablespoons
- Garlic powder – 2 tablespoons

THE SMOKE

- Preheat the electric smoker to 225°F (110°C)
- Add maple smoker wood chips

METHOD

1. Add the butter, fresh lemon juice, lemon pepper seasoning and garlic powder to a microwave-safe bowl.
2. Microwave for 30 seconds or until the butter is entirely melted, stir to combine.
3. Arrange the crab legs on the smoke for approximately 35 minutes, basting with the melted butter mixture every 10 minutes.
4. When 25 minutes have elapsed, move the crab legs nearer to the smoker's heat source and smoke for 2 minutes, on each side. The crab lets should be charred on the outer shell. The total smoking time for the crab legs is approximately half an hour.
5. Remove from the smoke and serve.

ALE-BRINED CATFISH WITH CILANTRO LEMON DIPPING SAUCE

TOTAL COOK TIME 2 HOURS 40 MINUTES

INGREDIENTS FOR 3 SERVINGS

THE FISH

- 3 whole catfish, cleaned and headed
- Olive oil – 1 tablespoon
- Seafood seasoning, to taste

THE BRINE

- Belgian triple ale – 1½ cups
- Kosher salt – ⅛ cup
- 1 fresh lemon
- Yellow mustard – 1 teaspoon
- Water – 2 cups

THE DIPPING SAUCE

- Mayonnaise – 1 cup
- 1 green onion, top only
- Cilantro, chopped – 2 tablespoons
- Hot sauce – 1 teaspoon
- Freshly squeezed orange juice – 2 teaspoons
- Salt – ⅛ teaspoon
- Cracked black pepper – ⅛ teaspoon

THE SMOKE

- Preheat the electric smoker to 265°F (130°C)
- Add orange smoker wood chips

METHOD

1. First, prepare the brine by combining the ale with the salt and juice in a bowl, stirring until the salt is entirely dissolved.
2. Add the mustard and stir.
3. Transfer the catfish to a large ziplock bag. Add sufficient water to cover the fish, seal the bag and place in the fridge for 60 minutes.
4. After 60 minutes have elapsed, remove the fish from the brine. Discard the brine.
5. Using kitchen paper towel, pat the fish dry.
6. Rub the oil all over the fish and season with the seafood seasoning.
7. Place the fish in the smoker.
8. While the fish smokes, prepare the dipping sauce.
9. In a bowl, combine the mayonnaise with the onion, cilantro, hot sauce, freshly squeezed orange juice, salt, and black pepper. Transfer to the fridge until needed.
10. Smoke the fish until it registers 145°F (65°C). This will take approximately 1 hour 5 minutes.
11. Remove the fish from the electric smoker and allow to rest for 10 minutes.
12. Serve the smoked catfish with a side order of dipping sauce.

MUSSELS IN WINE BROTH

TOTAL COOK TIME 55 MINUTES

INGREDIENTS FOR 2 SERVINGS

THE SEAFOOD

- Fresh mussels, scrubbed, picked over (2.2-lbs, 1-kgs)

THE INGREDIENTS

- Unsalted butter – 4 tablespoons
- Olive oil – 1 tablespoon
- Shallots, minced – 2 tablespoons
- 1 garlic cloves, peeled, minced
- Flat leaf Italian parsley – 2 tablespoons
- Dry white wine - ½ cup
- 1 rosemary twig
- 1 thyme twig
- French baguette, sliced, to serve

THE SMOKE

- Preheat the electric smoker to 145°F (65°C)
- Pre-soaked pecan wood chips work well
- Use a fine grate to avoid the scallops falling through

METHOD

1. First, clean the mussels by scrubbing them in lots of cold water to remove any debris.
2. Using a knife, sharply tap any open mussels and discard any that don't close.
3. Remove the beards and place the prepared mussels in a bowl of fresh, cold water until ready to use. You will need to change the water a few times depending on how long you intend to wait before smoking them.
4. Using a small sharp knife cut off the top shells of the mussels, discard, and soak the mussels in the broth.
5. When you are ready to smoke, filter the liquid through a kitchen paper towel and set aside.
6. Put the mussels in foil and place them in the electric smoker for 30 minutes.
7. The mussels are ready when their shells open.
8. Meanwhile, prepare the sauce: Add the butter along with the olive oil to pan and melt.
9. Add the shallots followed by the garlic and cook for 3 minutes.
10. Bring the heat to a high temperature and pour in the white wine, cooking for 2-3 minutes, until it begins to reduce.
11. Reduce the heat to a simmer and add the sprigs of rosemary and thyme.
12. When both the mussels and sauce are cooked, add the mussels to a bowl.
13. Pour the wine sauce over the top and garnish with parsley.
14. Serve with slices of French bread.

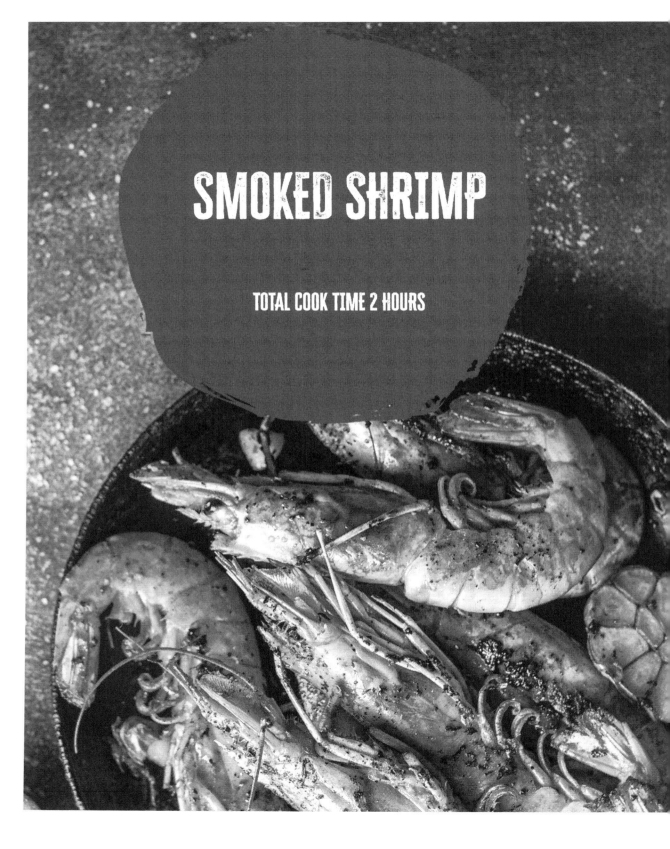

SMOKED SHRIMP

TOTAL COOK TIME 2 HOURS

INGREDIENTS FOR 4 SERVINGS

THE SEAFOOD

- Medium-size shrimp, peeled, deveined, washed (2-lbs, 0.9-kgs)

THE INGREDIENTS

- Uncooked grits – 1 cup
- Cream cheese, cubed (0.6-ozs, 1.70-gms)
- Velveeta cheese, cubed (0.4-ozs, 115-gms)
- Worcestershire sauce – 1 tablespoon
- 3 cloves garlic, peeled and minced
- Salt – 1 teaspoon
- Black pepper – ¼ teaspoon
- Smoked paprika – 1 teaspoon
- Dijon mustard – 1 teaspoon
- 1 medium egg, well beaten
- Butter, melted – ½ cup
- Garlic powder – 1 teaspoon
- Onion powder – 1 teaspoon
- Cajun seasoning – 1 teaspoon

THE SMOKE

- Preheat the electric smoker to 225°F (110°C)
- Fill the water bowl, to half capacity with orange juice
- Add alder smoker wood chips to the tray or loader

METHOD

1. Cook the grits according to the package directions.
2. While the grits are hot, stir in the cream cheese along with the Velveeta cheese, Worcestershire sauce, minced garlic, salt, black pepper, smoked paprika, and Dijon mustard. Add the egg and stir to combine.
3. Transfer the grits to an aluminum foil covered disposable aluminum pan.
4. Heat a small pot, add the butter along with the garlic powder, onion powder, and Cajun seasoning. Stir thoroughly to combine.
5. Place the shrimp in an aluminum pan and pour the butter-cajun seasoning over the top.
6. Smoke both of the pans for 45 minutes.
7. Remove both pans from your smoker and carefully drain off all of the excess butter from the shrimp pan.
8. Arrange the grits on a plate and top with the shrimp.
9. Serve and enjoy.

SMOKED PULLED BOAR ON MAC N' CHEESE

TOTAL COOK TIME 6 HOURS 35 MINUTES

INGREDIENTS FOR 1-2 SERVINGS

THE MEAT
- Wild boar shoulder (5-lbs, 2.3-kgs)

THE BRINE
- Water (1-gal, 4-lts)
- Sugar – 1 cup
- Kosher salt – 1 cup
- Black peppercorns – 1 tablespoon
- 1 bunch of fresh thyme, washed
- 1 head of garlic, peeled, halved
- 1 bunch of fresh parsley, washed

THE RUB
- Smoked paprika – 1 cup
- Brown sugar – ¼ cup
- Celery salt – ½ cup
- Granulated garlic – 3 tablespoon
- Cayenne pepper – 1 teaspoon
- Freshly ground black pepper – 1 teaspoon
- Salt – ½ teaspoon

THE SAUCE
- Ketchup – 1 cup
- Apple cider vinegar – 1 cup
- 4 chipotle peppers in adobo sauce
- Brown sugar – 3 tablespoons
- Sea salt – ½ teaspoon

THE MAC N' CHEESE
- Butter – 3 tablespoons
- All-purpose flour – ¼ cup
- Salt – ½ teaspoon
- Black pepper – ¼ teaspoon
- Whole milk – 2 ½ cups
- Macaroni noodles (8-ozs, 230-gms)
- Cheddar cheese, grated – 3 cups
- Chives, to garnish

THE SMOKE

- Preheat the electric smoker to 250-275°F (120-135°C)
- Pecan or mesquite wood chips are recommended for this recipe

METHOD

1. For the brine: In a large stockpot, bring the water to simmer. Add the sugar along with the kosher salt, and bring to boil while stirring to incorporate and entirely melt the sugar and salt. Remove the pot from the heat.
2. Next, add the peppercorns followed by the thyme, garlic, and parsley. Allow the water to come to room temperature, before transferring to the fridge to chill.
3. For the rub, in a bowl combine all the ingredients (smoked paprika, brown sugar, celery salt, granulated garlic, cayenne pepper, black pepper, and salt).
4. For the sauce: Combine all the ingredients (ketchup, apple cider vinegar, chipotle pepper, brown sugar, and sea salt) in a food processor and process until silky smooth. Simmer in a pan over low heat for 10 minutes.
5. Season the meat with the spice rub and place it in the smoker. Smoke until it reaches an internal temperature of 180°F (80°C). This will take between 3-4 hours.
6. Shred the meat and toss evenly in the barbecue sauce.
7. For the Mac n' Cheese: Over moderate heat, in a pan, add the butter to melt.
8. Once melted, add the flour followed by the salt and black pepper and whisk for 2-3 minutes.
9. Continue whisking and gradually in a steady stream, pour in the milk, while continuing to stir for 10-12 minutes, until the sauce thickens.
10. Cook the pasta in a pan of boiling water until al dente. Drain and rinse in cold water.
11. Combine the drained pasta with the cheese sauce.
12. Top the Mac n' Cheese with the cooked meat, and garnish with chopped chives.

SMOKED DUCK

TOTAL COOK TIME 6 HOURS 45 MINUTES

INGREDIENTS FOR 4 SERVINGS

THE MEAT

- 1 whole duck (5-lbs, 2.3-kgs)

THE MARINADE

- Red wine vinegar – ¾ cup
- Soy sauce – ¾ cup
- Runny honey – ¾ cup
- Garlic salt – 2 tablespoons
- Freshly ground black pepper – 2 tablespoons

THE SMOKE

- Preheat the electric smoker to 250°F (120°C)
- Add a 50/50 mix of water and apple juice to the water

METHOD

1. In a bowl, combine the marinade ingredients (red wine vinegar, soy sauce, honey, garlic salt, and freshly ground black pepper). Stir to combine. Set ½ cup of the marinade aside.
2. Add the duck to a suitably sized re-sealable ziplock bag.
3. Pour the remaining ½ cup of marinade over the duck and transfer to the fridge for between 2-4 hours, to marinate.
4. Remove the duck from the marinade and place on the middle rack of your smoker for 60 minutes, basting 5-7 times with the reserved ½ cup of marinade.
5. When the duck is well browned, cover the bird with aluminum foil and continue smoking for between 2½-4 hours, or until its internal temperature reaches 165°F (75°C).
6. Allow to rest and carve.

SMOKED PHEASANT

TOTAL COOK TIME 13 HOURS

INGREDIENTS FOR 8-12 SERVINGS

THE MEAT

- 2 whole peasant

THE BRINE

- Kosher salt – ¼ cup
- Brown sugar – ¼ cup
- Water – 4 cups

THE INGREDIENTS

- Pure maple syrup – 2 cups

THE SMOKE

- Preheat the electric smoker to 200°F (95°C)
- Choose either apple or hickory wood chips

METHOD

1. In a bowl, dissolve the salt along with the brown sugar in the water.
2. Arrange the pheasants in a bowl and cover with the brine. Adding additional water if needed to submerge.
3. Transfer the container to the refrigerator and allow to rest for 12 hours.
4. Remove the pheasants from the brine and using kitchen paper towel, pat dry and set on a cooling rack to dry for a minimum of 60 minutes.
5. Place the pheasants in the smoker.
6. Boil the maple syrup down and after 60 minutes, use it to baste the pheasants.
7. Continue basting every 30 minutes, until the pheasant registers an internal temperature of 165°F (75°C).
8. Remove the pheasants from the smoker.
9. Enjoy warm.

SMOKED BBQ WILD RABBIT

TOTAL COOK TIME 3 HOURS 30 MINUTES

INGREDIENTS FOR 2-3 SERVINGS

THE MEAT

- 1 cottontail rabbit, skinned and gutted

THE BRINE

- Kosher salt – 2 tablespoons
- White vinegar – ½ cup
- Water

THE RUB

- Garlic powder – 1 tablespoon
- Cayenne pepper – 1 tablespoon
- Salt – 1 tablespoon
- Freshly ground black pepper – 1 tablespoon
- 1 store-bought bottle of BBQ sauce

THE SMOKE

- Preheat the electric smoker to 200°F (93°C)
- Hickory wood chips are a good choice for this recipe

METHOD

1. Add the rabbit to a shallow dish.
2. For the brine: Dissolve the salt in the vinegar and pour it over the rabbit. Add sufficient water to cover and allow the rabbit to brine for a minimum of 60 minutes.
3. Take the rabbit out of the brine and pat dry.
4. Whisk equal parts of garlic powder, cayenne pepper, salt, and pepper in a bowl.
5. Liberally season the rabbit with the rub.
6. Add the rabbit to the smoker and smoke for 15 minutes. Mop the rabbit with the BBQ sauce, repeating every 15 minutes.
7. When 2 hours have elapsed, take the rabbit out of the smoker, mop with BBQ sauce, and serve.

VENISON JERKY

TOTAL COOK TIME 18 HOURS 10 MINUTES

INGREDIENTS FOR 15-18 SERVINGS

THE MEAT

- Venison, cut into strips (6-lbs, 2.7-kgs)

THE MARINADE

- Brown sugar – ½ cup
- Worcestershire sauce – ⅛ cup
- Garlic salt – ½ teaspoon
- Soy sauce – ½ cup
- Dry mustard – ½ teaspoon
- Salt – ¼ cup
- Dash of pepper
- Water – 3 cups

THE SMOKE

- Preheat the electric smoker to 140°F (60°C)
- Add mesquite or hickory smoker wood chips

METHOD

1. Add the brown sugar, Worcestershire sauce, garlic salt, soy sauce, dry mustard, salt, pepper, and water. Stir until combined.
2. Place the strips of venison in the marinade for 6 hours.
3. Remove the venison from the marinade and using kitchen paper towel, pat dry
4. Smoke for between 12-14 hours until leathery and dry.
5. Allow to cool before cutting into bite-sized scissors.

PORTOBELLO MUSHROOMS

TOTAL COOK TIME 2 HOURS 15 MINUTES

INGREDIENTS FOR 4-6 SERVINGS

THE VEGETABLES

- 12 large Portobello mushrooms, stemmed

THE INGREDIENTS

- Extra-virgin olive oil
- Sea salt and freshly ground black pepper
- Herbs de Provence
- Water, to fill

THE SMOKE

- Preheat the electric smoker to 200°F (95°C)
- Fill the water bowl to half full before adding the wood chips to the side tray

METHOD

1. First, clean the Portobello mushrooms by wiping them all over with a kitchen paper towel. Rub them all over with extra-virgin olive oil and season with salt and freshly ground pepper. Sprinkle the inside of the caps with Herbs de Provence.
2. Arrange the mushrooms, cap side facing downwards, directly on top of the grill rack.
3. Smoke the mushrooms for 2 hours. Refill the water in the bowl and tray 45-60 minutes into the smoking process.
4. Carefully remove the mushrooms so that the herbal juice inside the mushrooms caps doesn't spill out.

SMOKED BRUSSELS SPROUTS

TOTAL COOK TIME 2 HOURS 15 MINUTES

INGREDIENTS FOR 6-8 SERVINGS
THE VEGETABLES

- Brussels sprouts, rinsed and trimmed (1-lbs, 0.5-kgs)

THE INGREDIENTS

- Extra-virgin olive oil – 2 tablespoons
- 2 cloves garlic, minced
- Sea salt – 1 teaspoon
- Freshly cracked black pepper – ½ teaspoon
- Water, to fill

THE SMOKE

- Preheat the electric smoker to 250°F (120°C)
- Add the wood chips
- Fill the water bowl to halfway

METHOD

1. First, cut the Brussels sprouts in half, lengthwise.
2. Add the sprouts to a glass bowl and on high, microwave for 3 minutes. Set aside to cool for 2-3 minutes.
3. Add the olive oil, garlic, salt, and pepper in a mixing bowl and whisk until incorporated. Add the sprouts to the bowl and toss to coat evenly.
4. Add the sprouts to an ovenproof frying pan or cast iron skillet.
5. Position the skillet on the upper rack of your smoker and smoke for approximately 2 hours, until fork tender. Check the cooking progress after 1½ hours.
6. Serve and enjoy.

SMOKY SWEET POTATOES

TOTAL COOK TIME 2 HOURS 10 MINUTES

INGREDIENTS FOR 6 SERVINGS

THE VEGETABLES

- 6 sweet potatoes, scrubbed, eyes removed

THE INGREDIENTS

- Extra-virgin olive oil
- Sea salt
- Butter
- Black pepper

THE SMOKE

- Preheat the electric smoker to 250°F (120°C)
- Add the wood chips
- Fill the water bowl to halfway

METHOD

1. First, using a metal fork, pierce the unpeeled sweet potatoes several times. Brush them with olive oil and season with sea salt.
2. Position the potatoes on the top rack and smoke for between 2-3 hours, until fork tender and oozing.
3. Serve the potatoes slathered with butter and seasoned with salt and pepper.

In short, electric smokers have paved the way for every American to enjoy the delight of smoked meat from the comfort of their home. These electric smokers are, therefore, often advertised with the tagline "Set it and Forget It," which quickly gives an idea of the core functionality of the appliance. Electric smokers quickly provide the option to smoke meats through an easy-to-use and accessible interface. Since modern electric smokers are packed with intelligent software, the smoker monitors the temperature throughout the smoking process without requiring human involvement. All you have to do is set it up and allow the smoker to do its magic!

SMOKING MEAT BASICS

FOOD SAFETY

BASIC FEATURES

Smokers from different brands are bound to have some tricks, some features almost staple to every electric smoker. Having a good knowledge of these base features will give you a clear idea of what you are going into!

CONSIDERABLY SPACIOUS: Most Electric Smokers are usually very spacious to allow you to smoke meat for a large group of people. Generally speaking, the size of the Electric Smoker ranges from 527 square inches to 730 square inches.

LIGHT WEIGHT: Regular charcoal smokers are bulky and even tough to move! Modern Electric Smokers tend to be highly soft in weight, which makes them easier to move and very mobile. An average Electric Smoker usually weighs somewhere around 40-60 pounds. The inner walls of the smokers are made of stainless steel, which makes them lightweight and durable.

CONSTRUCTION: Normally, most Electric Smokers, are built with durability kept in mind. The design of an Electric Smoker and the ergonomics are often designed with very high-quality imported materials that give it a very long-lasting and safe build. These appliances are 100% safe for both you and your family.

CHROME COATED RACKS: Bigger-sized smokers are often divided into 2-4 compartments that are fully plated with a high-quality chrome. These racks are very easy to remove and can be used to keep large pieces of meat without making a mess. Even the most basic electric smokers tend to have at least four chrome-coated racks.

EASILY CLEANABLE: As Electric Smokers are getting increasingly advanced, they are also becoming more accessible and easy to use. The Stainless Steel walls mean you can easily smoke your meat and veggies and easily clean the smoker afterward.

SAFE TO USE: Electric Smokers are generally built with much grace and don't pose any harm. However, a degree of caution is always to be kept. As long as you follow the guidelines and maintain proper safety procedures, there's no risk of accidental burns or electric shocks from a smoker.

THE BASIC STEPS

Now, the good news for all of your smoke enthusiasts is that using an Electric Smoker isn't rocket science! It means anyone can use it, following some basic and simple guidelines. So it would be best to go through this section before smoking your meat. After all, you don't want your expensive cut to be ruined just because of some silly mishap, right?

Just follow the basics, and you will be fine!
- The first step is to make sure that you always wear safety gloves
- Take out the chips tray and add your wood chips (before smoking begins)
- However, once the smoking has started, you can easily use the side chip tray to add your chips
- The additional chips are required to infuse the meat with a more smoky flavor
- Once the chip bay is ready, load up your marinated meat onto the grill directly
- The stainless steel rack is made for direct smoking; however, if you wish, you can use a stainless steel container to avoid drippings
- Once the meat is in place, lock the door of the chamber
- Turn your smoker "On" using the specified button and adjust the temperature
- Wait until it is done!

Remember that the abovementioned steps are merely basic; different recipes might require additional steps. Either way, they won't be much complicated as, well!

YOUR FIRST ELECTRIC SMOKER

Buying an Electric Smoker is by no means an easy investment. They are generally quite expensive and require a lot of effort and dedication to get one. Due to the sheer variety of Electric Smokers though, it sometimes gets really difficult for an individual to find and purchase the one that is best for their needs. Especially if that individual is a complete beginner in this field. I wanted to make sure that you don't fall victim to such an event, as the feeling of making an unsatisfactory purchase is all but joyful! Therefore, in the following section, I have broken down the key elements that you should keep an eye out for while making your first Electric Smoker purchase. After this section, you will also find a list of the Top 10 Electric Smoker (At the time writing) that your money can buy! That being said, here are the factors to consider.

PRICE: This is perhaps the most decisive part of your purchase. Always make sure to do a lot of research in order to find the best one that falls within your budget (the provided list will help you). However, you should keep in mind that going for the cheapest one might not be a good idea!

As much tempting as they might sound, the quality of the build materials and the finished meal won't be up to mark.

Asides from that, things to keep in mind include
- The reviews
- Safety ratings
- Warranty of the device

CAPACITY: Electric smokers come in different sizes, and you are bound to find one that will suit your need. Before purchasing your Electric Smoker, the things that you should consider in terms of capacity include the following:

- Decide the place where you are going to keep your smoker and hot it will be stored
- Assess the size of your family and how much meat you are going to cook in each batch

Depending on your smoking experience, you will need a larger-capacity smoker if you tend to throw a lot of events! But if it's for personal use, a reasonably small one will do.

BRAND: At the time of writing, Bradley and Masterbuilt were at the forefront of the Electric Smoker market. However, some other brands include Smoke Hollow, Esinkin, and Char-Broil.

A good idea is to not rely on a brand too much but rather look at the specific models and assess the one that suits your needs (depending on the features of the smoker)

DURABILITY: Always keep the device's durability (even if it costs an extra dollar)!

As mentioned earlier, a Smoker is an expensive investment, and you want to buy one that will last you for years.

Two of the most significant issues when it comes to durability that you should keep in mind are

- The quality of the thermostat
- Quality of the seal

If your smoker is properly sealed up, it will require less heat to control and prevent the smoke from escaping and will allow the veggies and meat to be penetrated by the smoke evenly, giving more delicious meals.

SAFE AND ACCESSIBILITY: Even though you are an experienced smoker or a beginner, always read through every single functionality of the smoker that you are considering. Read the provided manufacturer's guide to better educate yourself on the smoker and assess how safe and accessible the smoker might be for you. (According to your experience level)

BARBECUING AND SMOKING MEAT

You might not believe it, but there are still people who think that the process of Barbequing and Smoking are the same! So, this is something you should know about before diving deeper. So, whenever you use a traditional BBQ grill, you always put your meat directly on top of the heat source for a brief amount of time which eventually cooks up the meal. Smoking, on the other hand, will require you to combine the heat from your grill as well as

the smoke to infuse a delicious smoky texture and flavor into your meat. As a result, smoking usually takes much longer than traditional barbecuing. In most cases, it takes a minimum of 2 hours and a temperature of 100 -120 degrees for the smoke to be properly infused into the meat. Keep in mind that the time and temperature will depend on the type of meat you are using, which is why it is suggested to keep a meat thermometer handy to ensure that your meat is doing fine. Also, remember that this barbecuing method is also known as "Low and slow" smoking. With that cleared up, you should be aware that there are two different ways smoking is done.

COLD AND HOT SMOKING

Depending on the type of grill that you are using, you can get the option to go for a Hot Smoking Method or a Cold Smoking One. However, the primary fact about these three different cooking techniques which you should keep in mind are as follows:

- **HOT SMOKING**: In this technique, the food will use both the heat on your grill and the smoke to prepare your food. This method is most suitable for chicken, lamb, brisket, etc.

- **COLD SMOKING**: In this method, you are going to smoke your meat at a very low temperature, such as 85 F (30 degrees Celsius), making sure that it doesn't come into direct contact with the heat. Cold smoking is mainly used

- **ROASTING SMOKE**: This is also known as Smoke Baking. This process is essentially a combined form of roasting and baking and can be performed in any smoker with a capacity to reach temperatures above 180 F (80 degrees Celsius).

SELECTING A SMOKER

You need to invest in a good smoker if you smoke meat regularly. Consider these options when buying a smoker. Here are two natural fire options for you:

- **CHARCOAL SMOKERS**: are fueled by a combination of charcoal and wood. Charcoal burns quickly, and the temperature remains steady so you won't have any problem with a charcoal smoker. The wood gives a great flavor to the meat, and you will enjoy smoking meat.
- **WOOD SMOKER:** The wood smoker will give your brisket and ribs the best smoky flavor and taste, but it is harder to cook with wood. Both hardwood blocks and chips are used as fuel.

DIFFERENT SMOKER TYPES

You should know that in the market, you will get three different types of Smokers

CHARCOAL SMOKER

These smokers are hands down the best for infusing the perfect smoky flavor to your meat. But be warned that these smokers are difficul2t to master as the method of regulating temperature is a little bit difficult compared to standard Gas or Electric smokers.

ELECTRIC SMOKER

After the charcoal smoker, next comes the more straightforward option, Electric Smokers. These are easy-to-use and plug-and-play types. All you need to do is plug in, set the temperature, and go about your daily life. The smoker will do the rest. However, remember that the smoky finishing flavor won't be as intense as the Charcoal one.

GAS SMOKERS

Finally, comes the Gas Smokers. These have a reasonably easy temperature control mechanism and are usually powered by LP Gas. The drawback of these Smokers is that you will have to keep checking up on your smoker now and then to ensure that it has enough Gas.

DIFFERENT SMOKER STYLES

The different styles of Smokers are essentially divided into the following.

VERTICAL (BULLET STYLE USING CHARCOAL)

These are usually low-cost solutions and are perfect for first-time smokers.

VERTICAL (CABINET STYLE)

These Smokers have a square-shaped design with cabinets and drawers/trays for easy accessibility. These cookers come with a water tray and a designated wood chips box.

OFFSET

These types of smokers have dedicated fireboxes that are attached to the side of the main grill. The smoke and heat required for these are generated from the firebox, which is passed through the main chamber and out through a nicely placed chimney.

KAMADO JOE

And finally, we have the Kamado Joe, which ceramic smokers are largely regarded as being the "Jack of All Trades." These smokers can be used as low and slow smokers, grills, high or low-temperature ovens, and so on.

They have a thick ceramic wall that allows them to hold heat better than any other smoker, requiring only a little charcoal.

These are easy to use with better insulation and are more efficient when it comes to fuel control.

comes to fuel control.

CHOOSE YOUR WOOD

You need to choose your wood carefully because the type of wood you will use affect significantly to the flavor and taste of the meat. Here are a few options for you:

- **MAPLE**: Maple has a smoky and sweet taste and goes well with pork or poultry
- **ALDER**: Alder is sweet and light. Perfect for poultry and fish.
- **APPLE**: Apple has a mild and sweet flavor. Goes well with pork, fish, and poultry.
- **OAK**: Oak is great for slow cooking. Ideal for game, pork, beef, and lamb.
- **MESQUITE**: Mesquite has a smoky flavor and is extremely strong. Goes well with pork or beef.
- **HICKORY**: Has a smoky and strong flavor. Goes well with beef and lamb.
- **CHERRY**: Has a mild and sweet flavor. Great for pork, beef, and turkey

The Different Types Of Wood	Suitable For
Hickory	Wild game, chicken, pork, cheeses, beef
Pecan	Chicken, pork, lamb, cheeses, fish.
Mesquite	Beef and vegetables
Alder	Swordfish, Salmon, Sturgeon and other types of fishes. Works well with pork and chicken too.
Oak	Beef or briskets
Maple	Vegetable, ham or poultry
Cherry	Game birds, poultry or pork
Apple	Game birds, poultry, beef
Peach	Game birds, poultry or pork
Grape Vines	Beef, chicken or turkey
Wine Barrel Chips	Turkey, beef, chicken or cheeses
Seaweed	Lobster, mussels, crab, shrimp etc.
Herbs or Spices such as rosemary, bay leaves, mint, lemon peels, whole nutmeg etc.	Good for cheeses or vegetables and a small collection of light meats such as fillets or fish steaks.

CHARCOAL

In General, there are three different types of charcoal. All of them are porous residues of black color made of carbon and ashes. However, the following are a little distinguishable due to their specific features.

- **BBQ BRIQUETTES:** These are the ones that are made from a fine blend of charcoal and char.

- **CHARCOAL BRIQUETTES:** These are created by compressing charcoal and are made from sawdust or wood products.

- **LUMP CHARCOAL:** These are made directly from hardwood and are the most premium quality charcoals. They are entirely natural and are free from any form of additives.

RIGHT TEMPERATURE

- Start at 250F (120C): Start your smoker a bit hot. This extra heat gets the smoking process going.

- Temperature drop: Once you add the meat to the smoker, the temperature will drop, which is fine.

- Maintain the temperature. Monitor and maintain the temperature. Keep the temperature steady during the smoking process.

Avoid peeking now and then. Smoke and heat are the two crucial elements that make your meat taste great. If you open the cover every now, and then you lose both of them, and your meat loses flavor. Only open the lid only when you truly need it.

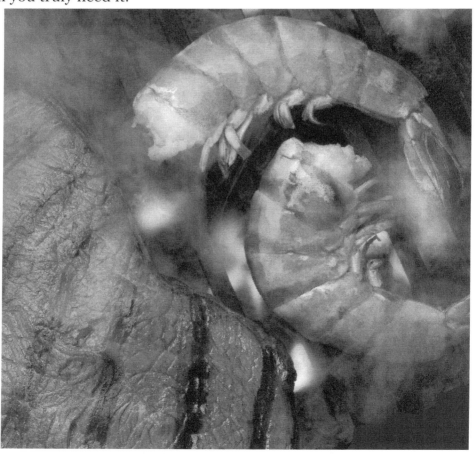

BASIC PREPARATIONS

- Always be prepared to spend the whole day and take as much time as possible to smoke your meat for maximum effect.
- Ensure you obtain the perfect Ribs/Meat for the meal you are trying to smoke. Do a little bit of research if you need.
- I have already added a list of woods. Consult that list and choose the perfect wood for your meal.
- Make sure to prepare the marinade for each of the meals properly. A great deal of the flavors comes from the rubbing.
- Keep a meat thermometer handy to get the internal temperature when needed.
- Use mittens or tongs to keep yourself safe.
- Please refrain from using charcoal infused alongside starter fluid, as it might bring a very unpleasant odor to your food.
- Always start with a small amount of wood and keep adding them as you cook.
- Don't be afraid to experiment with different types of wood for newer flavors and experiences.
- Always keep a notebook near you and note jot down whatever you are doing or learning and use them during future sessions. A notebook will help you to evolve and move forward.

ELEMENTS OF SMOKING

Smoking is a very indirect method of cooking that relies on many factors to give you the most perfectly cooked meal you are looking for. Each component is essential to the whole process as they all work together to create the meal of your dreams.

- **TIME**: Unlike grilling or even Barbequing, smoking takes a long time and requires a lot of patience. It takes time for the smoky flavor to get infused into the meats slowly. Just to compare things, it takes about 8 minutes to thoroughly cook a steak through direct heating, while smoking (indirect heating) will take around 35-40 minutes.

- **TEMPERATURE:** When it comes to smoking, the temperature is affected by many factors that are not only limited to the wind and cold air temperatures but also the cooking wood's dryness. Some smokers work best with large fires that are controlled by the draw of a chimney and restricted airflow through the various vents of the cooking chamber and firebox. At the same time, other smokers tend to require minor fire with fewer coals and a completely different combination of the vent and draw controls. However, most smokers are designed to work at temperatures as low as 180 degrees Fahrenheit to as high as 300 degrees Fahrenheit. But the recommended temperature usually falls between 250 degrees Fahrenheit and 275 degrees Fahrenheit.

- **AIRFLOW:** The air to which the fire is significantly exposed determines how your fire will burn and how quickly it will burn the fuel. For instance, if you restrict airflow into the firebox by closing up the available vents, the fire will burn at a low temperature and vice versa. Typically in smokers, after lighting up the fire, the vents are opened to allow for maximum airflow and are then adjusted throughout the cooking process to ensure that optimum flame is achieved.

- **INSULATION:** Insulation is also essential for smokers as it helps to manage the cooking process throughout the whole cooking session. Good insulation allows smokers to reach the desired temperature instead of waiting hours!

FOOD SAFETY

CLEANLINESS OF THE MEAT

If you can follow the steps below, you will be able to ensure that your meat is safe from any bacterial or airborne contamination.

This first step is essential as no market-bought or freshly cut meat is entirely sterile.

Following these would significantly minimize the risk of getting affected by diseases.

- Make sure to properly wash your hands before beginning to process your meat. Use fresh tap water and soap/hand sanitizer.
- Make sure to remove metal ornaments such as rings and watches from your wrist and hand before handling the meat.
- Thoroughly clean the cutting surface using sanitizing liquid to remove any grease or unwanted contaminants. If you want a homemade sanitizer, you can simply make a solution of 1 part chlorine bleach and ten parts water.
- The sanitizer mentioned above should also be used to soak your tools, such as knives and other equipment, to ensure that they are safe to use.
- Alternatively, commercial acid based/ no rinsed sanitizers such as Star San will also work.
- After each use, all knives and other equipment, such as meat grinders, slicers, extruders, etc., should be cleaned thoroughly using soap water. The knives should be taken care in particular by cleaning the place just on top of the handle as it might contain blood and pieces of meat.
- When cleaning the surface, you should use cloths or sponges.

A note of sponges/clothes: It is ideal that you keep your sponge or cleaning cloth clean as it might result in cross-contamination. These are ideal harboring places for foodborne pathogens. Just follow the simple steps to ensure that you are on the safe side:

- Make sure to clean your sponge daily. It is seen that the effectiveness of cleaning it increases if you microwave the dam sponge for 1 minute and disinfect it using a solution of ¼ -1/2 teaspoon of concentrated bleach. This process will kill 99% of bacteria.
- Replace your sponge frequently, as using the same sponge every time (even with wash) will result in eventual bacterial growth.
- When not using the sponge, please keep it dry and wring it off of any loose food or debris.

KEEPING YOUR MEAT COLD

Mismanagement of temperature is one of the most common reasons for outbreaks of foodborne diseases. The study has shown that bacteria grow best at temperatures of 40 to 140 degree Fahrenheit/4-60 degree Celsius, which means that if not taken care of properly, bacteria in the meat will start to multiply very quickly. The best way to prevent this is to keep your meat cold before using it. Keep them eat in your fridge before processing them and make sure that the temperature is below 40 degrees Fahrenheit/4 degree Celsius.

KEEPING YOUR MEAT COVERED

All foods start to diminish once they are opened from their packaging or exposed to the air. However, the effect can be greatly minimized if you cover or wrap the foods properly.

The same goes for meat.

Good ways of keeping your meat covered and wrapped include:

- Using aluminum foil to cover up your meat will help to protect it from light and oxygen and keep the moisture intact. However, since Aluminum is reactive, it is advised that a layer of plastic wrap is used underneath the aluminum foil to provide a double protective coating.
- If the meat is kept in a bowl with no lid, then plastic wrap can seal the bowl, providing an airtight enclosure.
- Re-sealable bags protect by storing them in a bag and squeezing out any air.
- Airtight glass or plastic containers with lids are good options as well.
- A type of paper known as Freezer paper is specifically designed to wrap foods to be kept in the fridge. These wraps are excellent for meat as well.
- Vacuum sealers are often used for Sous Vide packaging. These machines are a bit expensive but can provide excellent packaging by completely sucking out any air from a re-sealable bag. This greatly increases the meat's shelf life outside and in the fridge.

PREVENTING FORMS OF CROSS-CONTAMINATION

Cross-Contamination usually occurs when one food comes into contact with another. In our case, we are talking about our meats.

This can be avoided very easily by keeping the following things in check:

- Always wash your hands thoroughly with warm water. The cutting boards, counters, knives, and other utensils should also be cleaned as instructed in the chapter's first section.
- Keep different types of meat in separate bowls, dishes, and plates before using them.
- When storing the meat in the fridge, keep the raw meat, seafood, poultry, and eggs on the bottom shelf of your fridge and in individual sealed containers.
- Keep your refrigerator shelves cleaned, and juices from meat/vegetables might drip on them.
- Always refrain from keeping raw meat/vegetables on the same plate as cooked goods.
- Always clean your cutting boards and use different cutting boards for different foods. Raw meats, vegetables, and other foods should be cut using a different table.

KNIVES

KNIVES: Sharp knives should be used to slice the meat accordingly. While using the knife, you should keep the following in mind.

- Always make sure to use a sharp knife
- Never hold a knife under your arm or leave it under a piece of meat
- Always keep your knives within visible distance
- Always keep your knife point down
- Always cut down towards the cutting surface and away from your body
- Never allow children to toy with knives unattended
- Wash the knives while cutting different types of food

Index

CONCLUSION

I am happy to share this cookbook with you, and I take pride in offering you an extensive array of recipes that you will love and enjoy. I hope you benefit from each of our recipes, and I am sure you will like all the recipes we have offered you. Don't hesitate to try our creative and easy-to-make recipes, and remember that I have put my heart into coming up with delicious meals for you. If you like my recipes, you can share them with acquaintances and friends. I need your encouragement to continue writing more books!

P.S. Thank you for reading this book. If you've enjoyed this book, please don't shy; drop me a line, leave feedback, or both on Amazon. I love reading feedback and your opinion is extremely important to me.

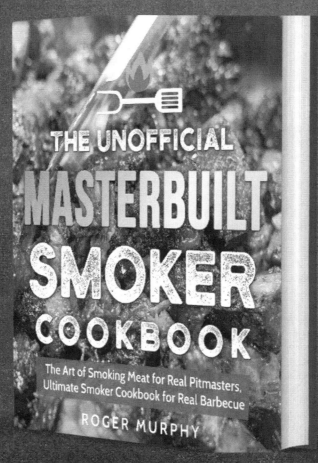

Made in the USA
Columbia, SC
27 April 2025

57217094R00072